PARASITES

The Ebola Virus

Shelley Bueche

KIDHAVEN PRESS™

THOMSON
★
GALE

San Diego • Detroit • New York • San Francisco • Cleveland
New Haven, Conn. • Waterville, Maine • London • Munich

THOMSON

GALE

Picture Credits
Cover: © CDC/Science Photo Library
© AFP/CORBIS, 8, 19, 24
AP/Wide World Photos, 11, 21
CDC/C. Goldsmith, 6 (inset), 27
CDC/Dr. Fred Murphy, 12 (inset)
COREL Corporation, 6
© B. Dowsett, CAMR/Photo Researchers, 5

Chris Jouan, 18
© David Phillips/Visuals Unlimited, 16 (left)
PhotoDisc, 26 (left)
© Science Source/Photo Researchers, 15
© Science VU/CDC/Visuals Unlimited, 21 (inset)
© SIU/Visuals Unlimited, 12, 16
© Dr. Paul A. Zahl/Photo Researchers, 26

© 2004 by KidHaven Press. KidHaven Press is an imprint of The Gale Group, Inc.,
a division of Thomson Learning, Inc.

KidHaven™ and Thomson Learning™ are trademarks used herein under license.

For more information, contact
KidHaven Press
27500 Drake Rd.
Farmington Hills, MI 48331-3535
Or you can visit our Internet site at http://www.gale.com

LIBRARY OF CONGRESS CATALOGING-IN-PUBLICATION DATA

Bueche, Shelley.
  Ebola / by Shelley Bueche.
    v. cm. — (Parasites)
Includes bibliographical references and index.
Contents: The ebola virus as a parasite—The ebola virus attacks—Stories in the 'hot
zone'—Preventing future ebola outbreaks and working toward finding a cure.
  ISBN 0-7377-1780-7
  1. Ebola virus disease—Juvenile literature. [1. Ebola virus disease. 2. Virus diseases.
3. Diseases.] I. Title. II. Series.
  RC140.5.B84 2004
  616.9'25—dc21
                                                                    2003009613

Printed in China

CONTENTS

The Ebola Virus as a Parasite

Ebola is a type of **virus** that causes a serious disease. A virus is a **parasite**. Parasites feed or depend on another organism to live. A parasite lives off its host without offering anything in return. All viruses are parasites. Viruses **infect** everything that lives, including animals, plants, and **bacteria**. Viruses can be found in land, water, or even in air.

Once inside a human or animal cell, viruses multiply. Yet in animals and humans, viruses can stay inactive for a long time, only to become active years later. Today more than five hundred different viruses attack human cells. Once a virus moves inside a body, it spreads easily and can make the

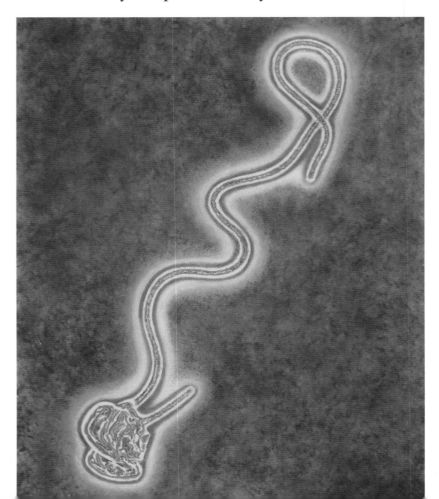

The parasitic Ebola virus causes serious disease in animals and people.

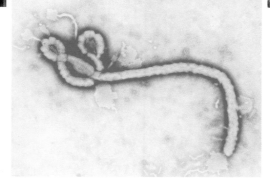

The first case of Ebola (inset) was discovered in the Democratic Republic of Congo (shown) in 1976.

host sick. A virus can multiply so fast that a trillion copies of the virus can be found in one drop of blood. More viruses could appear in that drop of blood than there are stars in the sky.

Viruses and bacteria cause infectious diseases. They kill 13 million people yearly. Some viruses are not that serious and can cause people to become sick with colds or flu. Other viruses are more deadly. One of these killer viruses is the Ebola virus.

The Ebola Virus

Ebola is named after the Ebola River near Yambuku, the Democratic Republic of Congo (formerly Zaire), in Africa where the first case of the disease was found. Although Ebola was first **identified** in 1976, most researchers believe that Ebola has been around for much longer, perhaps hundreds of years. The virus has only just started to jump from animals to people. Luckily it is also a very rare virus and outbreaks are usually contained in one area. Ebola **hemorrhagic** fever, the disease caused by the Ebola virus, can kill up to nine out of every ten people infected with it.

Ebola is mysterious. Doctors are still researching and finding out how to treat persons who have been infected. Because the virus kills its victims faster than the virus can spread, **outbreaks** are usually limited to small areas and last only a short time. Ebola mainly attacks health care workers and family members treating infected patients.

Ebola is one of a group of hemorrhagic viruses. These viruses are found only in humans and monkeys. These viruses cause hemorrhagic fever with massive bleeding inside of the body. The Ebola virus can go from monkeys to humans and hide away for years between outbreaks.

Relatives of Ebola victims, standing outside a hospital, shield their faces during an outbreak of the virus.

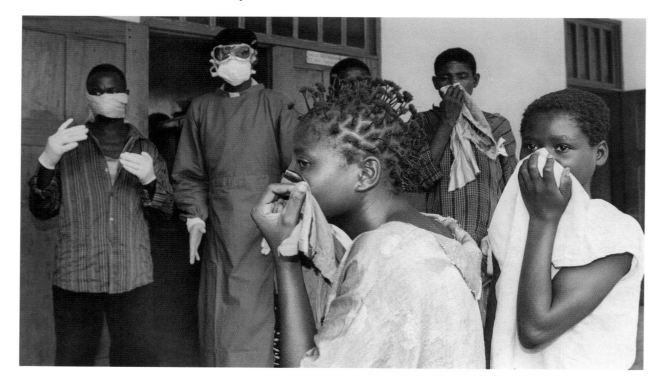

Ebola hemorrhagic fever occurs in the Democratic Republic of Congo, Gabon, Sudan, Nigeria, Cameroon, Ivory Coast, Kenya, and the Republic of the Congo in central Africa. Not one human case of Ebola has occurred in the United States.

Ebola disease can spread through the body fluids of an infected person. It is a weak virus, and once outside of a body, Ebola needs to find another host or it dies right away. Ebola does not travel through the air, though it spreads and attacks the body extremely quickly.

CHAPTER 2

The Ebola Virus Attacks

The Ebola virus is most often spread through personal contact. Usually the infection spreads among hospital staff or family members caring for a patient or loved one. Blood, body fluids, and dirty needles are responsible for passing the virus. The virus spreads quickly in poor nations, where hospitals are often **primitive**. Hospitals in central Africa lack fresh water and items necessary for proper germ control such as rubber gloves and gowns. Moreover, these hospitals can become so overcrowded that several patients may share one bed. Under these conditions, the virus can spread easily.

Symptoms

Ebola attacks a person's **immune system**. The immune system tries to fight the virus. A person

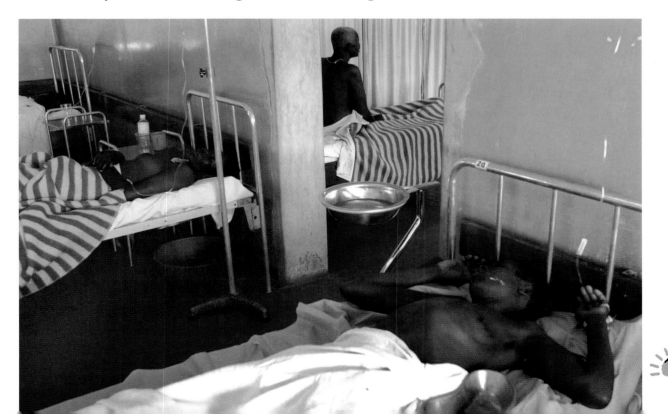

Ebola patients lie in bed. Ebola spreads quickly in primitive hospitals like this one.

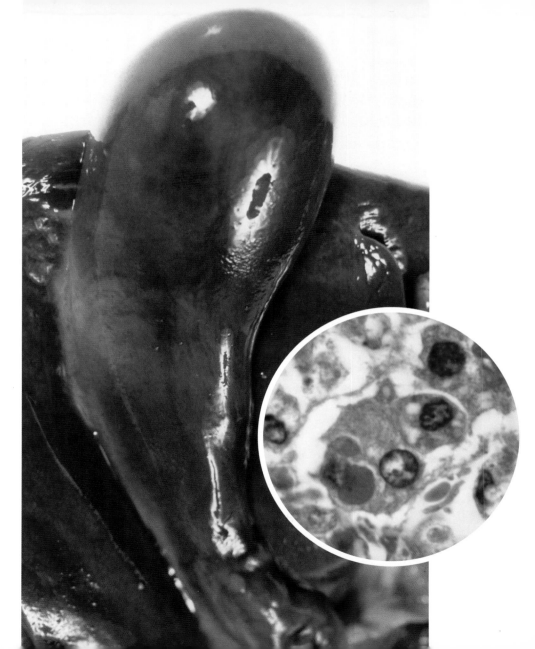

Ebola infects every organ in the body, including the liver (inset) and gall bladder (both pictured right).

who is exposed to Ebola can go from two to twenty-one days before the virus begins to attack the body. Once the virus attacks, it does a lot of damage in a short period of time. An infected person first experiences headaches, fever, and body pain, then begins to violently throw up. The virus travels through the body attacking all of the organs, including the heart, liver, skin, lungs, and brain. The only parts of a person's body that are not destroyed by Ebola are muscles and bones. After the virus travels the body, a person becomes weak and dizzy and loses his or her sense of balance.

In the first few days after being infected, a person will have a high fever, muscle pain, red eyes, a sore throat, and a rash. Small holes show up in the blood vessels. Then small blood clots begin to appear in the bloodstream. The infected person's mouth, nose, ears, and eyeballs bleed, and the heart bleeds back into itself. The person begins to throw up blood with black spots filled with the virus. The virus attacks and turns every part of the body into liquid slime.

The virus also attacks the brain. Once this happens, infected people become confused, sometimes angry, and scared. Ebola patients often become forgetful and try to run away from their hospital beds. Many Ebola patients try to fight with the doctors and loved ones who are caring for them.

As the blood infected with the virus travels throughout the entire body, it begins oozing through the skin, making painful blisters. A terrible rash appears. Red spots on the skin become huge bruises. The skin becomes soft and can rip like paper. By the time the virus has done its damage, death usually follows from shock and heart failure. The process is over within one to two weeks.

There is no medicine for Ebola patients. Patients need plenty of rest, fluids, and food. Doctors and nurses try to reduce fever and pain in their patients and treat any infections.

Survivors

A small number of people infected with Ebola survive. Doctors think that survivors of Ebola have

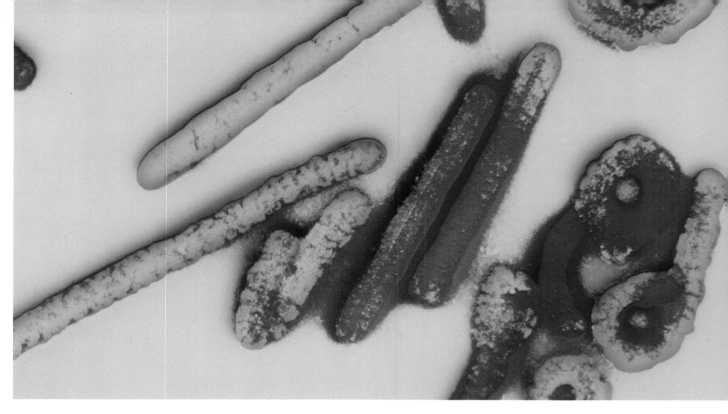

stronger immune systems than those who die of the disease. The lucky few that survive usually take from two to five weeks to get better.

Once patients have recovered, they are no longer infectious. However, because Ebola can be so deadly with such terrifying symptoms, survivors are often feared by others and left alone. Health officials travel

The Ebola virus (pictured) attacks the brain, causing the patient to feel afraid and confused.

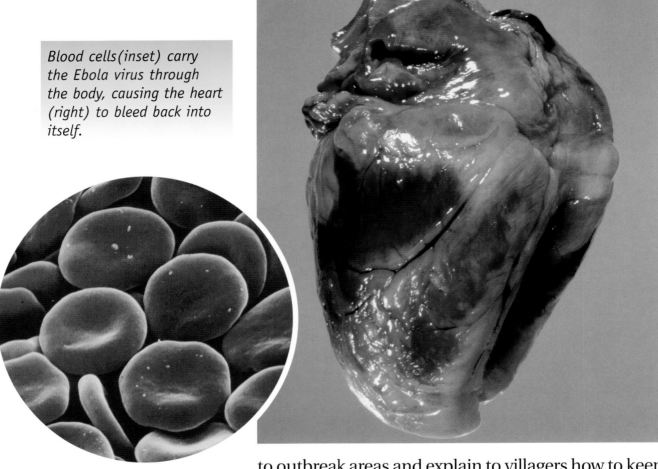

Blood cells(inset) carry the Ebola virus through the body, causing the heart (right) to bleed back into itself.

to outbreak areas and explain to villagers how to keep from catching the disease. These workers also try to help others know that survivors of Ebola are not **contagious** and do not have to be avoided by others.

Stories in the "Hot Zone"

The Ebola virus is very contagious and deadly. Since 1976 more than 1,700 people have been infected and 1,150 people have died from the disease. Here are the stories of some people infected with Ebola.

Dr. Matthew

Dr. Matthew Lukwiya, a forty-three-year-old medical doctor, worked with the World Health Organization in Africa. He traveled to the Democratic Republic of Congo to care for Ebola patients. Seventeen people in the village had already died there. One night Dr. Matthew worked with Sister Maria, a nurse, caring for patients. "Blood was pouring from his nose and eyes like tap water," said one of the health care workers of the patient they were treating. "He started to become

Ebola Outbreaks

A F R I C A

Sudan

Nigeria

Republic of the Congo

Ivory Coast

Cameroon

Atlantic Ocean

Ebola River

Kenya

Gabon

Democratic Republic of the Congo

Indian Ocean

※ Site of first known Ebola outbreak, 1976

Countries with known Ebola outbreaks

confused, fighting death tooth and nail. He started pulling out his tubes, trying to leave the ward, so we called Dr. Matthew."[1] Dr. Matthew quickly put on a mask, cap, gown, apron, and two pairs of gloves, but forgot to cover his eyes with goggles.

Hospital workers wear face masks and gloves while transporting a coffin containing an Ebola victim. The virus is highly contagious.

He was sick with Ebola symptoms just one week later.

Dressed in a space suit covering her whole body, Dr. Matthew's wife, Margaret, visited her husband. She started to cry, but he told her if she cried, she would start to rub her face, which would not have been safe. Even as he was dying, Dr. Matthew thought of others instead of himself.

Dr. Matthew was buried with the other Ebola victims near the hospital. Margaret said of Dr. Matthew, "I don't think he would regret this. He saw what was needed for his patients and he did it. That was him."[2]

Adamou

Adamou, a five-year-old boy who lived in central Africa, died of Ebola. He was the fifth person in his family to die from Ebola. His mother, a nurse, died after treating an infected patient.

"My heart is heavy. I can't cry anymore. If I do, everything will fall apart,"[3] John Otolany, Adamou's uncle, said.

Otolany was the only one in the family able to put his nephew in a small plastic body bag after he died. The boy's uncle then sprayed the grave with germ killers and lowered the body into the family grave site.

Nurse Mayinga

Nurse Mayinga was a beautiful, twenty-year-old African woman. She had been caring for Sister M.E.,

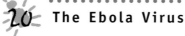

a nun who was sick with Ebola. Mayinga did not know how she caught the virus, but she got a terrible headache and was too tired to worry about what was wrong with her. She left the hospital and disappeared.

Health care workers bury the body of five-year-old Adamou after the boy died of Ebola (inset).

For two days, she wandered in town in a daze. She felt worse. She was then admitted to the hospital where she used to work. Although well cared for and kept in **quarantine**, she died. Although Mayinga could have unknowingly infected others, she did not.

James Akena

Many in James Akena's village considered him lucky; after all, he survived Ebola. Yet he was feared by his fellow villagers. When Akena came home, he found it had been burned to the ground. He had no money and no home. His neighbors were scared of him and ignored him. They feared he was an evil spirit.

Akena ended up living in an abandoned bus. He was starving. The village health workers tracked him down and helped him. The workers gave Akena help in moving away from his hometown of Gulu, where the Ebola outbreak had been.

CHAPTER 4

Prevention and the Hope for a Cure

Ebola is hard to stop once it has begun. One of the ways to keep it from spreading is to quarantine, or keep separate, people who have the disease. Anyone treating patients sick with Ebola must wear protective goggles, gowns, gloves, and masks. In African villages with Ebola, the local army comes in and closes all roads and schools to prevent people from entering or leaving the area.

A hospital worker dressed in protective clothing cleans a child's feet during an Ebola outbreak.

It used to be a custom in Africa to wash the dead body of a loved one before he or she was buried. But because so many African villagers are finding out about Ebola, this practice has been stopped. Now

when a person dies of Ebola in the hospital, the body is sealed in a special body bag and then buried. If someone dies of Ebola at home, local workers dressed in space suits covering the entire body, helmets, and rubber boots come to help the family seal the body in a plastic bag and bury it.

Doctors think that Ebola may be spread by contact with wild animals in the forest. Doctors think, for example, that monkeys may carry the disease. This is because hunters who ate a dead monkey came down with Ebola and spread the disease in 1996. Because Africans hunt and eat monkeys, doctors think they get the disease from them. Doctors are trying to educate Africans to change their hunting habits and not eat monkeys.

Finding a Cure

Researchers are also trying to find a cure for Ebola. They hope to do this by finding a **host**, an animal that carries the Ebola virus, but does not become sick. Doctors have found that some insect- and fruit-eating bats in Africa become infected but do not die. Scientists are studying these bats and

insects to find out more about Ebola and how it infects people.

By studying these animals and their immune systems, researchers hope to develop a **vaccine**. The National Institute of Health (NIH) has tested a vaccine on monkeys infected with the Ebola virus. The vaccine has been successful. The NIH will soon begin to test the vaccine in people to see

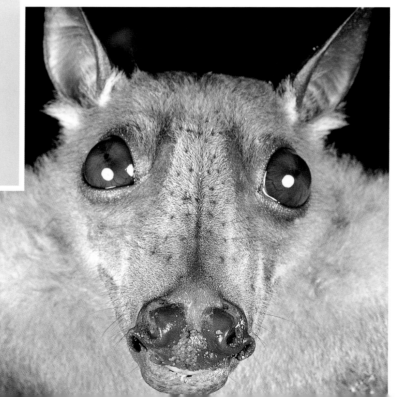

Scientists hope to find a cure for Ebola by studying animals that are immune to the virus, such as these African fruit-eating bats.

26

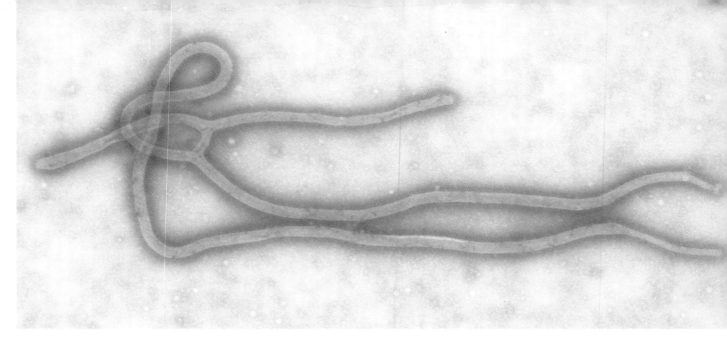

if it works. In the future, a successful vaccination might help the world get rid of the Ebola disease.

Ebola has the highest death rate and worst symptoms of any disease. There are still many questions about the Ebola virus waiting to be answered. These facts are why scientists are working so hard to prevent outbreaks around the world.

Education is the key to the control of disease. By telling others how to recognize the symptoms of Ebola and immediately isolating infected persons,

Understanding how the Ebola virus works is an important part of controlling the deadly disease.

an outbreak can be limited. It is also important for people to understand the symptoms of Ebola so that they can be treated as quickly as possible. With every outbreak, researchers learn more about Ebola and how to treat the disease.

Scientific discoveries, new medicine, and continued investigations are all very important in treating and controlling the Ebola virus. The many mysteries surrounding the virus make it difficult to find a cure. It is still difficult to find out where Ebola comes from and why it suddenly attacks. It will continue to hide in the rain forest, waiting to strike again, until a cure can be found.

Chapter 3: Stories in the "Hot Zone"

1. Quoted in James Astill, "The Death of Dr. Matthew," *Guardian*, January 2, 2001.
2. Quoted in Astill, "The Death of Dr. Matthew."
3. Alexandra Zavic, "Ebola Returns to Mekambo Village," Associated Press, January 7, 2002.

GLOSSARY

bacteria: Small germs that live almost everywhere in nature.

contagious: Something that is very likely to spread from one person to another.

hemorrhagic: Bloody.

host: A cell that has been infected by a virus is called the host cell of the virus.

identify: To find something out or to show something.

immune system: A part of your body that helps protect you from harmful germs and disease.

infect: When a germ passes from one person to another person.

outbreak: A disease that spreads in one area very quickly.

parasite: A virus that lives off another living thing without offering anything in return.

primitive: Not advanced or modern.

quarantine: The period of time when an infected person is kept alone or away from others who might catch the same disease. A whole town or hospital may be quarantined to keep germs from spreading.

vaccine: A shot of medicine given to prevent a certain disease.

virus: A tiny germ that invades animal, plant, and human cells and can cause disease.

Books

Don Nardo, *Germs*. San Diego, CA: KidHaven, 2002. An excellent book for beginning researchers. Explains differences between bad and good germs and tells how germs can actually help us. Wonderful photographs and charts to illustrate examples.

Katie Roden, *Plague*. Brookfield, CT: Copper Beach, 1996. A fun book with wonderful graphics.

Websites

Bigchalk.com (www.bigchalk.com). An online interactive guide for elementary students. Includes homework help. Go to keyword search: Ebola virus.

Centers for Disease Control and Prevention (www.cdc.gov). The international health agency headquarters are in Atlanta, Georgia. Look up Ebola virus. You will get the most recent facts at this site to use for reports.

HowStuffWorks.com (www.howstuffworks.com). This website analyzes the details of exactly how stuff works. Detailed information on viruses and how they work is included.

INDEX

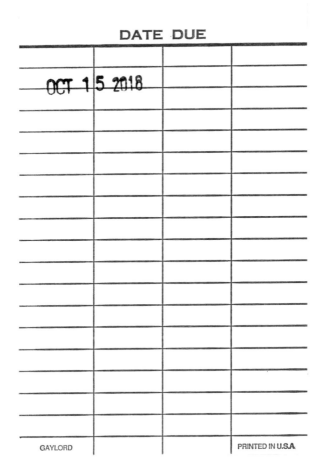

DATE DUE

OCT 15 2018			

GAYLORD · PRINTED IN U.S.A.